Dear Parent:

We're celebrating Columbus's arrival in the New World 500 years ago by sharing this original Weekly Reader Children's Book Club title with you.

There have been a lot of books about Christopher Columbus published recently. We feel *ours* is just right for the read-aloud set, who value pictures as much as clear, concise words.

Many people have been wondering: Was Columbus the actual discoverer of the Americas? Was he really a great man? Author Eric Arnold has written an honest story. Although Christopher Columbus may not measure up to 1990s standards, one of Columbus's greatest accomplishments was **overcoming fear of the unknown,** a lesson for all of us.

Hats off to Christopher Columbus! We hope you and your child make some discoveries together as you read this book.

Sincerely,

Stephen Fraser

Stephen Fraser
Senior Editor
Weekly Reader Books

Weekly Reader Children's Book Club Presents

Christopher Columbus:

Sailing the Sea of Darkness

By Eric Arnold

Illustrated by
Michael Malkovas

WEEKLY READER BOOKS · MIDDLETOWN · CONNECTICUT

For Christen and Tali
And to Rochelle, Ben and Adam
And to the memory of my parents, Esther and Irv

Steve Fraser – Thank you for your support and good humor
Ann Murphy – Thank you – We promise we'll write more

And to the Board of HOLE IN THE SOCK Productions
Thanks for your hard work
and
belief in giving kids a voice
Terry Payne Butler, Dick Dougherty, Carolyn Hansen, Dick Harris
Dom Varisco, John Welch, Beth Winship

This book is an original presentation of Weekly Reader Books.
Weekly Reader Books offers book clubs for children
from preschool through high school. For further
information write: **Weekly Reader Books,**
4343 Equity Drive, Columbus, Ohio 43228.

Newfield Publications is a trademark
of Newfield Publications, Inc.
Weekly Reader is a federally registered trademark
of Weekly Reader Corporation.
Printed in the United States of America.

Editor: Stephen Fraser
Art Director: Vickie Kelly
Designers: David L. Brady, Janet Kanca

ISBN #: 0–8374–0495–9

Christopher Columbus was born in 1451 in Genoa, Italy, a busy seaport on the Mediterranean Sea.

His father was a weaver and so was his grandfather. In those days, the son almost always followed in his father's footsteps.

But not Christopher.

He dreamed he would sail the seas to learn more about the world and explore faraway places.

I want to be a sailor and have a life of adventure, thought Christopher.

He would pretend he was off sailing on the great Sea of Darkness, as the Atlantic Ocean was known then. He wondered if there were sea monsters and strange creatures down below.

When Christopher was 10, he made his first sea voyage. At 13, he left his father's house to seek his fortune as a seaman. A Captain took him on as a cabin boy.

Christopher sailed up and down the coast of Italy on the Mediterranean Sea, trading goods and fighting pirates and terrible storms.

When Christopher was 25 years old, he was sailing near Portugal when all at once his ship was attacked by pirates! Christopher and his mates fought back but the ship went down in flames and his crewmates drowned.

Luckily, Christopher was a strong swimmer. He was wounded but he grabbed an oar that was floating by. He held on tight. That night he swam six miles to shore. He washed up on the beach near a fishing village on the southern coast of Portugal. The village people found him the next day and nursed him back to health.

When Christopher was well enough to travel,
he made his way to Portugal's greatest city, Lisbon.
Lisbon was the perfect city for Christopher. Many
explorers sailed from its port trying to find new trade
routes to the East, or the Indies, which included India,
China, and Japan. The Indies were believed to have
great wealth and lots of silk, spices, and gold—
lots and lots of gold.

But it was not easy to get to the Indies. People had to travel around Africa and then sail east.

Christopher believed he had a better idea. He thought he could reach the Indies much faster by sailing west over the Sea of Darkness.

When Christopher was 33, he thought he
was ready to try the voyage. He went to King John
of Portugal to ask him for ships and money to go
to the Indies.

Christopher was surprised by the King's answer.

The King said, "No!"

But Christopher was determined to make his trip
to the Indies.

So, he went to meet with the King and Queen of Spain.

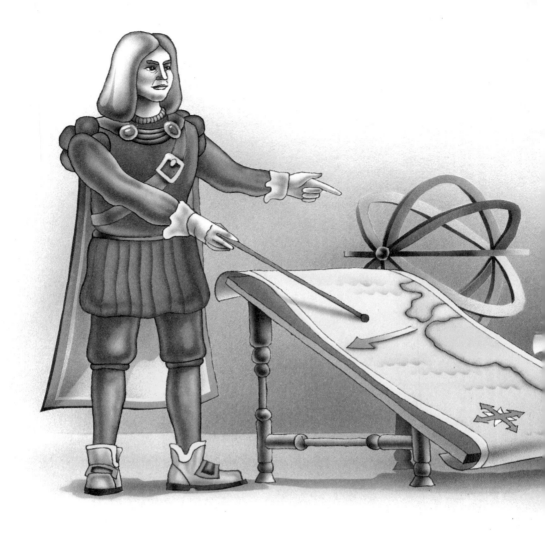

Isabella, the queen of Spain, wanted all the
people of Spain to be of the same Christian religion.
Christopher promised Queen Isabella not only riches
and fame but that he would convert, or change, the people
of the Indies to be Christians.

Christopher waited and waited for the Queen to
give him an answer.

"Yes," the Queen finally said—six years later!

Christopher wanted the Queen to make some
promises. If the voyage was a success, Christopher
wanted to be knighted and to be given the title of Admiral
of the Ocean Sea. He wanted to be made governor of all
the lands that he discovered, and given a part of all the
treasures he brought back to Spain.

The Queen thought this was a lot for Christopher
to ask but she decided she had nothing to lose.

Christopher thought he had everything to gain.

On **August 3, 1492,** Christopher set sail from Spain. He had three ships. They were the *Niña,* the *Pínta,* and the *Santa María.* Christopher sailed on the *Santa María,* which was the largest of the three.

Christopher brought food, water, wine, firewood, and guns for the journey. He also brought glass beads, bells, red caps, mirrors, and needles to trade for gold with the people of the Indies.

About 90 crew members were on board.
There were three doctors, in case somebody got sick.
There was even a marshal who was the police officer.
There were royal clerks, who were to write down
everything that happened on the journey and keep track
of what riches were brought aboard. Lots of cats were
brought on board to get rid of the rats that were
always found on ships.

Christopher was the captain of the entire fleet.

Day after day, there was nothing but water as far
as the eye could see. The crew became afraid because
they had never been out of sight of land for so long a time.

There were terrible storms; some of the men got
sick. Some died.

The crewmen became so upset with Christopher
for leading them into this dangerous and unknown sea
that they wanted to do away with him.

By early October, the crews wanted to turn around.

"Adelante! Adelante! (Onward! Onward!)"
cried Christopher.

Finally, two and a half months later, land was
sighted. Christopher went ashore in an armed boat to greet
the people. He called them Indios or Indians because
he was sure he had reached the Indies.

He named the beautiful island San Salvador.

The people he met were the Arawak Indians.
Christopher was surprised to see that they were not
wearing any clothes. They had gold rings in their
noses and ears. They couldn't understand
why Christopher and his crew *were* wearing
clothes and were so pale in color.

Christopher thought the people would make fine servants and could easily be made into Christians. But first he wanted to know where the gold mines were.

He made his way to Colba, or Cuba, as it is called today. *This isn't Japan!* he thought. *This must be China.* This too was a beautiful island.

"But where's the gold?" Christopher still wanted to know.

The Indians told Christopher of still another great island.

In December, he went there and it was the most beautiful island of all. It reminded him of Spain and he called it La Isla Española, or Hispaniola which means the "Island of Spain".

The people of Hispaniola had given him gifts which had a little gold in them. Christopher wanted to find the mines where this gold came from.

·CUBA·

·SA

So, he set sail again, but the *Santa María* shipwrecked on a coral reef.

The island people were very helpful unloading the ship's cargo.

I'll build a fort with the timber of the Santa María, Christopher thought. *I'll leave volunteers and supplies so they can gather gold. I'll come back later with more ships and more men to gather the gold and the spices.*

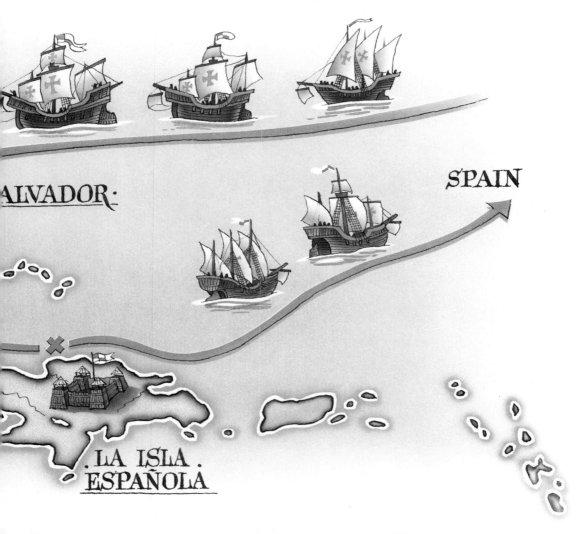

ALVADOR·

SPAIN

LA ISLA
ESPAÑOLA

Christopher set sail for Spain with the *Niña* and the *Pínta*.

The King and Queen gave Christopher a royal welcome. He told them he had found the Indies and showed off the gifts he brought back.

It was **June 1493** when Christopher set sail for his second voyage to the Indies.

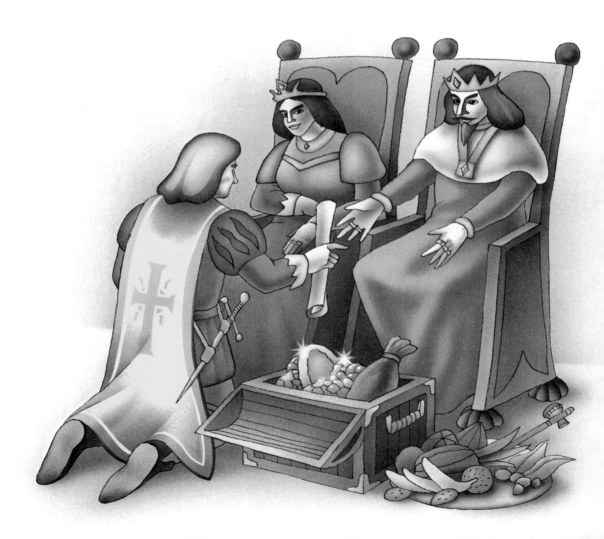

This time Christopher had 17 ships and more than 1,000 men. He also had farmers, soldiers on horseback, six priests, guard dogs and a supply of farm animals and grain.

The mounds of gold will be waiting for us! he thought, on the deck one evening as he looked at the stars.

He arrived at Hispaniola to visit the fort and
count his gold.

But he saw that the fort was burned down and
all the volunteers were dead. The men he left behind
had acted badly and fought with the Indians.

He set off to find another site on the island and
build a new fort. He named it Isabella after the Queen.

"We came to the New World for gold," said one upset
seaman. "Not to clear land or dig canals and build a new fort!"

Meanwhile, Christopher went to Cuba to look for gold. He found some but not nearly the amount he wanted or needed.

He did a lot of thinking. *Maybe I am not really in the Indies. Perhaps I didn't really find China or Japan! Could my whole trip be a mistake?*

He had promised the King and Queen that he would send some ships back to Spain with treasures right away. But he had hardly enough gold to send.

Christopher tried to get the Indians to look
for gold for him.

But not enough gold was found and Christopher,
himself, had to go back to Spain and talk with the
King and Queen.

He explained all that had happened to him
and his men over the last two years and eight months.

"Go back and try again!" the King and Queen said.

On **May 30, 1498,** Christopher set sail for his third voyage.

This time he headed south and explored the island of Trinidad and the continent of South America. These were new lands to Christopher but they still were not the Indies.

But if I'm not in the Indies, where am I? he thought. *I must be in the Garden of Eden!*

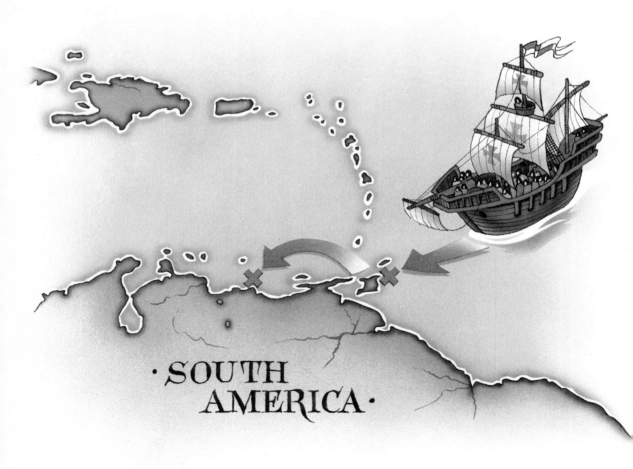

· SOUTH AMERICA ·

Trouble was waiting for him back in Hispaniola.

Terrible diseases were spreading and the men were
unhappy. Some didn't want to be in the New World anymore.
They hated being ruled by Christopher.

The King and Queen heard about the problems Christopher was having. They sent a new governor to find out what was wrong.

The new governor didn't like what he saw and he arrested Christopher on the spot.

Christopher was a very sad man when he returned to Spain.

Did people think he hadn't done a good job as an explorer and as a governor?

He wanted to prove them wrong.

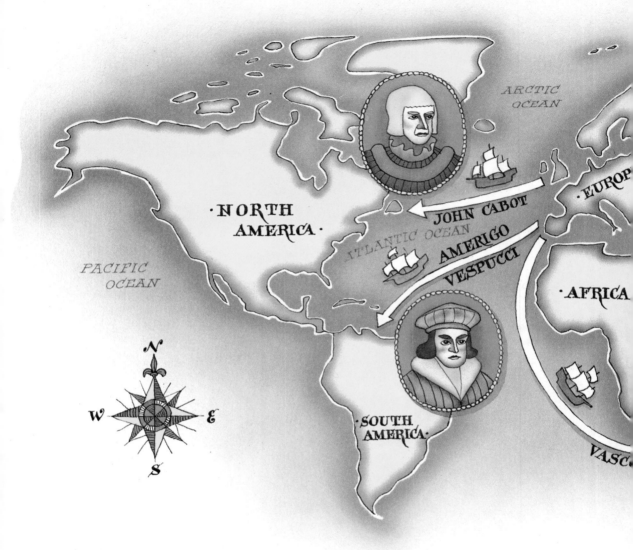

Meanwhile other explorers were sailing
their ships to "his" Indies.

John Cabot made it all the way to what is
now called Newfoundland, Canada in **1497.**

Amerigo Vespucci sailed to South America in
1501. He became so well known that "Amerigo" was
the word "America" is taken from.

And **Vasco da Gama** is the explorer who really

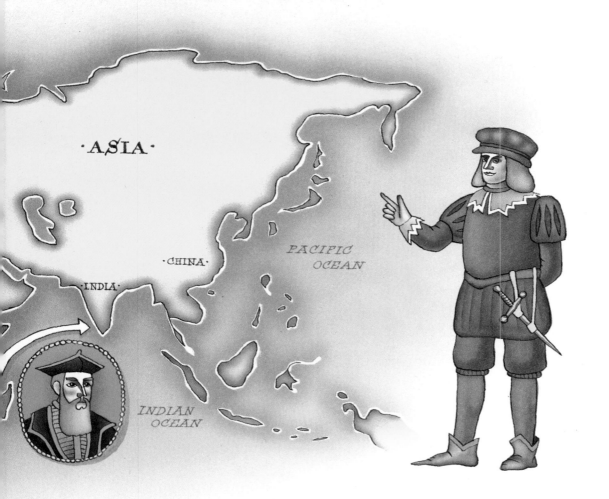

did make it to the Indies in **1498.** He made it to India
by sailing around the Cape of Good Hope of Africa.

This proved to the world that Christopher never
really made it to the Indies after all.

"I want one more chance to set sail!"
said Christopher as he paced his room one night.
"Vasco da Gama is still going the long way. I know
I can find a passage to the Indies. From there it will
only be ten days to India!"

The King and Queen agreed to give Christopher
his chance and on **April 3, 1502,** he set sail.

He called this trip the "High Voyage."

He looked for the passage in what is now
called Central America and explored where Honduras,
Nicaragua, Costa Rica, Panama, and Jamaica are today.

Christopher never found the passage to the Indies.

What he did was help explorers find the
courage to sail the great Sea of Darkness.